Library And Archives Canada Cataloging- in Publication Data

Danielle Bailey Poetics- A Prophetic Poetry Devotional On Life, Love, And Relationships To Help Keep You Spiritually Fit!

Published by: UNQLY MADE, LLC

Cover Design by:
IBC Graphics Atelier Studios
(410) 305-9450
IBCgraphicsinc@gmail.com

ISBN-13:978-0995859418
ISBN-10:0995859418

DEDICATION

I'd like to dedicate this book to my first love; God. You have graced me and given me favor to write prophetic poetry. Without you, none of this would have been possible and I am thankful that you have chosen me to fulfill this assignment.

Forever grateful and eternally yours.

Sincerely,

Your daughter and faithful servant,
Danielle

CONTENTS

INTRODUCTION

This prophetic poetry devotional was inspired by God and written by me with the leading and guidance of the Holy Spirit. The objective of this devotional is to encourage, transform, inspire, ignite, renew, realign, edify, and educate by planting the right seeds into the minds of the readers who want change and desire growth in the area concerning all facets of their lives. Too often poetry is written off as boring, unimportant, tedious, redundant and minuscule. However, many of the greats or dare I say legends have written poetic pieces that had eventually become the great ballads that we all know and love today; for instance the Psalm of David, Song of Solomon, Bob Marley, and Tupac Shakur just to name a few. The collection of poetry that has been written has embodied what thus sayeth the Lord. The profound depth in which it entails truly exemplifies how much we need to dig deeper and touch on the root of the problem we see here in this world and in the body of Christ. It needs to be addressed and I have been chosen for such a time as this to speak and share what the Lord has led me to say to you his people, in a poetic, eclectic and unqly made way.

My poetry really isn't just my poetry it is the prophetic downloads in which I have received from the Most High God Elohim El' Shaddai to rhyme with a unique cadence, symmetry and flow unlike any other. I am just a willing and able vessel who prayed and asked God to be used in a mighty way however the Lord deemed fit. It was said by the Lord in Habakkuk 2:2-3 "And the LORD answered me, and said, Write the vision, and make it plain upon tables, that he may run that readeth it. For the vision is yet for an appointed time, but at the end it shall speak, and not lie: though it tarry, wait for it; because it will surely come, it will not tarry". The Lord gave me the vision to write this on time and in season prophetic devotional. It was through my obedience that God knew that he could trust me to follow through with what he has instructed me, and by my doing so I have now been able to bless many fearfully and wonderfully made people with prophetic prophecies, edifying words of encouragement and warning. I pray that you will be blessed by the poetry in this book called, Poetics- A Prophetic Poetry Devotional: On Life, Love, And Relationships To Help Keep You Spiritually Fit!

PART ONE

~

HEAVENLY FATHER

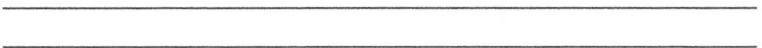

YOUR LOVE (Prayer Song)

God, your love is what I want
God, your love is what I need.

God, your is what we want
God, your love is what we need.

As I lift my hands and give praise to the Most High
Oh, Father give me strength to face another day to
get me through these ending of days,
to get me through these ending of days.

Oh, God we give you praise each and everyday
because you are worthy to be praised.

Amen.

Thank you, Heavenly Father.

THE VOICE

The voice inside says that it won't be denied
the living word of God has my mind hypnotized,
feels like there's a million and one things on my
mind I have to remember to take it one day at a
time.

Never forgetting who I was, but needing to
understand and embrace whom I'm becoming;
losing the wants, needs or urge to enjoy what was
never intended to be had.

Finally seeing the entirety of God's plan for me, my
life, is to see me working for his kingdom and all of
its Glory with all that I am and all my might.

Even in the still of the night, I can hear a voice that
says, "You can do all things through Christ who
strengthens you".

Never to leave my side for he is my God; My
shield, my buckler, my protector, Amen.

Reflection Section

Write your thoughts down to express
how the poem made you think or feel.
Then reflect on them to see what you
can do to make a difference.

_____

_____

_____

_____

_____

_____

_____

_____

_____

_____

_____

_____

_____

_____

_____

_____

_____

ALPHA & OMEGA

The Alpha and the Omega is the author and finisher, the complete of my soul, the captain of my life and the anchor of my spirit he orders my steps wherever he needs me to go.

There's nothing like the love of Christ how he died for my sins, all to give my life a chance while visiting this world within, trying my very best to emulate and be just like him.

God means the absolute infinite to me,
wide as the ocean and deep as the sea
with the breath of life in my lungs
I hear the beat of my heart like the sound of 10,000 drums.

So grateful.

He was wounded for our transgressions and bruised for our iniquities.

Jesus, If I have ever disappointed you, please Father, forgive me.

Reflection Section

Write your thoughts down to express how the poem made you think or feel. Then reflect on them to see what you can do to make a difference.

_____

_____

_____

_____

_____

_____

_____

_____

_____

_____

_____

_____

_____

_____

_____

_____

_____

_____

PROPHETIC SCRIBE

Everybody wants to win a prize
but what have you really done to receive?
Better think twice yes, I'm talking about those
seeds. Don't you know that you'll reap what you
sow? Which makes you wonder where you will go.

While blessings are great rest assured I agree
But doing what is good and right is too, have you
ever met your neighbors need? Or were you too
into yourselves focusing on your own selfish
greed? Striving to be Christ like, will you ever get
the degree?

Perfectly imperfect that is what I'd like to think,
at least I'm not faking, I'm only being me on a
mission being about my Father's business
winning souls is the ultimate goal you see.

There's just too many people trying to fit into the
obvious glorified sin, living in the present because
they haven't thought about they're eternity will
they ever get in and meet the Holy King?

Have I began to pull on your heart strings?

The thought provoking prophetic poetry is truly only a warning of what is to come if you do not heed.

I need to speak only what the Most High gives me, I hope you all are listening as your sweat starts glistening from the word of the Lord, are you knees buckling?

For on the day of the Yahweh's return every knee will bow and every tongue will confess that Jesus is Lord and Savior of the World; but, by then it'll be too late for one's distress you had many chances to pass his tests.

Yes, I decree and declare this in Yahweh's name,

My God,
Amen.

Reflection Section

Write your thoughts down to express how the poem made you think or feel. Then reflect on them to see what you can do to make a difference.

_____

_____

_____

_____

_____

_____

_____

_____

_____

_____

_____

_____

_____

_____

_____

ELOHIM

Elohim El Shaddai he is truly one of a kind
his miracle, signs, and wonders still always blows
their minds; Yes, he lives and reigns I'm talking
about the Most High he's not a regular guy
the Alpha and Omega sits on the throne of grace.

We only dream of the day that we'll get to see his
face not living in the destruction of the human race,
the Lord's return draw nigh no one knows the time
whether it'll be day or night, prepare as he has
went on to prepare a new heaven and earth for us.

Where is the trust? We can't argue, we cannot fuss.
Love thy neighbor even our fellow stranger,
how can we say we love a God we've never seen,
but have we really been the best human beings
to the people that we see on a regular basis?

I'm trying to make it past all the bases and get that
home run.

Our brothers and sisters are dying please put down
the guns, you think its funny, you think its fun;
those are real caskets, that is real blood.

What does prosper a man to gain the world and to lose his soul? Instead of being a role model some of you chose to chase the gold follow after sin and forsake righteousness, but, in Christ it's pricelessness.

How do we forget or better yet consciously choose to disrespect God and all that he's done perhaps you don't remember that he sent his only son (amnesia).

It was never his intention for his creation to live our lives like Cain did Abel it's not like we're not able to think and make the right decisions. Can't you see that I have the incision, I was cut from a different cloth, decided to live a life of purpose not one of a sinful sloth.

Turning it around so that the King can be proud because on that day of judgment what will you say that you weren't given the same amount of chances that you had just yesterday, his mercies are renewed daily...

So, tell me what did you do with yours today?

Reflection Section

Write your thoughts down to express
how the poem made you think or feel.
Then reflect on them to see what you
can do to make a difference.

_____

_____

_____

_____

_____

_____

_____

_____

_____

_____

_____

_____

_____

_____

_____

_____

LISTEN

I digress nonetheless, those of them that choose to pretend and not accept will eventually come back scratching their heads wondering who, what, why and when.

I'm not your average every day woman, I truly am one of a kind, the sooner the better you'll realize that I have no need to speak no lies.

I am one with the one who created the skies but, for the simple fact your inner sides are disenfranchised towards my greater good.

Are you listening to my words?

If not, I really think that you should".

Peace Be Still...

Reflection Section

Write your thoughts down to express
how the poem made you think or feel.
Then reflect on them to see what you
can do to make a difference.

_____
_____
_____
_____
_____
_____
_____
_____
_____
_____
_____
_____
_____
_____

_____
_____

DEAR GOD,

In my darkest hour you protected me and kept me
safe, because I had the faith my heart was broken
and shattered with pain.

That was then it's no longer the same
I chose the rose like the lotus flower reign
to rise above those that tried to trample my fame,
they're mission to try and keep me insane.

You see my father The Alpha and Omega, the
beginning and end said to me daughter, please
check you friends they are not who they claim to be
they want you to meet your end, now, it couldn't be
any clearer I see it now more than ever.

Praise the Lord for severed relationships so sick
with contamination's filled with the infiltrations,
needed to invest in a new filtration systematic
automatic.

I have to be this diplomatic and be all that I know I
could be in a monopoly owned type of chess
played well God saved my life from the pits of hell.

He saw the best in me when nobody else would could it be that they never should, I believe that I was an outcast with men, so that I could be an in-cast with God.

In my darkest hour the Lord kept me safe and covered me with his mighty power filled blood, knowing that the vipers were out to bite me they tried to devour me, set a trap before me the trap in which they stumbled and fell in and rightfully so.

I wouldn't wish for they're demise, me?, oh no!

I leave that judgment to God alone because you see Jesus Christ has my heart and soul, for no weapons formed against me shall be able to prosper.

I never had to chase the fame I just walked in my purpose and glorified him in Jesus name, Amen.

The power of the anointing is in the power of the pain facing all the trials and tribulations was almost like some seriously calculated game, but I chose the rose like that lotus flower reign never to give into opposition ever again.

No, not me rising above the trials and tribulations is what I do best my friend or foe. The Father, The Son and The Holy Spirit are aligned like tic tac toe.

Either which way one thing's for sure I'm just letting you know that I will rise high and soar. Yes, I have to go preach and teach the masses this right here is all of life's classes in one and no it's not all fun.

The sky is the limit and mediocre thoughts are the floor, so what is it going to be I don't know about you, but I do know about me.

I was meant to rise high and see beyond the expectations that I was set out before me by mankind for they do not have a mind like mine.

"His thoughts are not our thoughts and his ways are not our ways, lean not on your own understanding and please listen to what I have to say".

God preserved me like Jonah in the season of isolation it was a mind awakening rejuvenation preservation.

I was so grateful for him keeping me away from the mediocre floor and kept me safe away in the secret place of his Tabernacle where I was able to seek him more.

Got mentally strong for the already prepared open doors, I can finally rise and soar high above like never before I literally humbled myself before the Lord and because of him I am able to do so much more.

Reflection Section

Write your thoughts down to express how the poem made you think or feel. Then reflect on them to see what you can do to make a difference.

_____

_____

_____

_____

_____

_____

_____

_____

_____

_____

_____

_____

_____

_____

_____

_____

PREACHER MAN

Preacher man, Preacher man why you such a creeper man why are you convicting yourself to hell in front of the people dem?

Preacher man, Preacher man stop sugar coating the scriptures dem, the time is at hand and your playing around like a foolish man.

Preacher man, Preacher man why you such a creeper man, don't you see God's plan at hand?

Preacher man, Preacher man why you such a creeper man. Are you okay with having the peoples blood on your hands?

Preacher man, Preacher man it's time for you to fix up man God is coming for his people dem, Preacher man, Preacher man it's time for you to change your ways and repent now man.

The Preacher man, The Preacher man is no longer a creeper man he's been toiling doing the work of the Lord.

Preacher man, Preacher man stand up tall and
reach them man. Preacher man, Preacher man use
your sword and save them man.

Yes, Preacher man, Preacher man now you're really
a saving man, saving his people of Yah;
Preacher man, Preacher man don't you feel better
man knowing that your preaching the word raw?

The Preacher man has redeemed himself,
he's truly an anointed Preacher man;
The Preacher man, Preacher man now he's a sold
out man, a sold out Man on fire for God.

Reflection Section

Write your thoughts down to express
how the poem made you think or feel.
Then reflect on them to see what you
can do to make a difference.

_____

_____

_____

_____

_____

_____

_____

_____

_____

_____

_____

_____

_____

_____

_____

_____

_____

PART TWO

~

LIFE

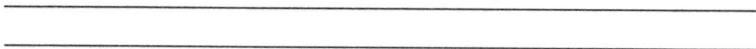

TOUCH NOT

Touch not his anointed and do his prophet no harm
is a direct order from our Lord Yeshua;
many times there has been modern day pharisees
ignoring the unction like the Egyptians they had no
function against the children of Israel.

The events that took place were definitely surreal
Pharaoh didn't believed in Moses and which God
he served to be real until he sent those plagues he
knew then for sure.

Touch not my anointed and do my prophets no
harm your asking for trouble when you disobey,
can you hear the alarms?

It doesn't matter whether you think God is a dream
believe it indeed or you'll have to relive what
Pharaoh was led to see.

Please remember he watches out and guides his
children even when they're backs were against the
wall he parted the red sea.

Listen carefully you had better heed, this is a warning to those that still seek to be used by the enemy.

He came to kill, steal and destroy but Jesus came that we may have life, and life more abundantly. I don't mind sounding repetitive, ever so redundantly.

Touch not his anointed and do his prophets no harm, yes he will lift up a standard against them; he upholds us with his righteous right arm
Ready for battle any day of the week, repent now and bow down to the Holy King's feet.

Reflection Section

Write your thoughts down to express
how the poem made you think or feel.
Then reflect on them to see what you
can do to make a difference.

_____

_____

_____

_____

_____

_____

_____

_____

_____

_____

_____

_____

_____

_____

_____

_____

THE PAST

Everyone has a PAST they maybe even lived it kinda fast, but that won't last we all have or had a chance to change it and rearrange it.

But instead of working on you, you choose to study me well if that's the case please kindly get on your knees and seek the Lords face instead of being a Dis(His)Grace.

Or should I say the body of Christ you gotta die to flesh daily in order to live this LIFE, in the Kingdom of God there is no more strife. What does it prosper a man to Gain the whole world and lose his Soul?

Me, personally I don't worship Silver and Gold! So, say what you want about me I take it as a compliment knowing that I chose to be a Son of God rather than Sons of Men. You can decide to be my Friend or secret Foe from way back when.

Either which way the Favor of the Lord still remains the same, this mostly because I still Glorify his wondrous Name.

His Mercy for me is tireless not because I'm a
Christian, but because I have a repentant heart, and
Jesus and I will Never part we've been together
from the very Start.

Everyone has a Past they maybe even lived it kinda
fast, but that won't last we all have a chance to
change it and rearrange it well at least before the
Lord returns I strongly suggest and advice you to
seek him while he can still be Found.

Don't worry about my past that's over and done
with, I live my life for the Lord and if you want to
fight with me I'll just use God's Sword which is his
Word, ya heard!!
Peace Be Still..

In Jesus name, Amen!!

Reflection Section

Write your thoughts down to express
how the poem made you think or feel.
Then reflect on them to see what you
can do to make a difference.

_____

_____

_____

_____

_____

_____

_____

_____

_____

_____

_____

_____

_____

_____

_____

_____

SIMPLICITY

They say that the eyes are the windows to the soul
as you look into them you have to ask yourself;
which way you'll go.

Mesmerized by the intensity of my heart and it's
simplicity, it shakes the quake of the hearts beating;
it's not fleeting or mistreating.

This love is unconditional!

The eyes are the window
The heart is the door
But, who do I hear creeping upstairs on the attics
floor (the mind)?

Could it be...

Is it a dream or is it that the rock of the waves is the
warmth of my tears streaming down on the inside
of my inner being, my face.

Reflection Section

Write your thoughts down to express
how the poem made you think or feel.
Then reflect on them to see what you
can do to make a difference.

_____

_____

_____

_____

_____

_____

_____

_____

_____

_____

_____

_____

_____

_____

_____

_____

KINGDOM BUSINESS

I look forward to the mental stimulation and self-proclamation, I possess a different type of sensation.

Let's all unite before they try to ruin the nation, together you and I we're going to educate the world and dominate the system.

Not tryna diss 'em, but they gonna have to listen, we follow the king by making the transition.

We're about the father's business, we suited up for the revival, so we got plenty of arch rivals, But God is almost on the arrival.

We're all here it's about the survival of the fittest,

Jesus is the illest, Satan's out here trying to kill us.

Thy Kingdom come, thy will be done on earth as it is in heaven. Yes, my favourite number is Seven, The enemy's just mad that he got kicked outta heaven.

Too bad so sad coulda, woulda, shoulda thought about that, it's a fact that he won't last..

got them talking 'bout The Lord, he's getting it ready to snap back and get it popping.

We all 'gon be stomping on the enemy's neck for the amount of times that he disrespects.

No weapons formed against us shall ever be able to prosper, for the Father the Alpha and the Omega Beginning and End reunites the lost souls as he fosters; his children for his big return.

Chastises the one's that he loves the most, with the Father, the Son and the Holy Ghost.

Reflection Section

Write your thoughts down to express
how the poem made you think or feel.
Then reflect on them to see what you
can do to make a difference.

_____
_____
_____
_____
_____
_____
_____
_____
_____
_____
_____
_____
_____
_____

_____
_____

PREGNANCY

Preganancy is something beautiful a wonderful
feeling, round, glowing, growing are the things
that you notice; happy, confused, overwhelmed is a
given.

Pregnant woman is you;

mother, daughter, sister, aunt.

Pregnancy is a blessing a gift from above,

 given to us as the chosen ones.

Be with child and be grateful for pregnancy is
something beautiful, a wonderful feeling.

Reflection Section

Write your thoughts down to express
how the poem made you think or feel.
Then reflect on them to see what you
can do to make a difference.

_____

_____

_____

_____

_____

_____

_____

_____

_____

_____

_____

_____

_____

_____

_____

_____

_____

GRACE

Once when I was lost and high I put a gun to my mind because I was blind, but, now I'm found I can finally see that God was always, has always been there with me.

To lead me out of the darkness when that enemy tried to play tricks on me it's hard to even remember, it's hard to even believe.

Taking part of things that wanted to employ me were the very things that was designed to destroy me, almost could have tried to decoy me it seemed as if I didn't care less; I m alloyed me.

When I was high I put the gun to my head I didn't pull the trigger or else I would've been dead But God! stuck closer than a brother, he was truly my friend.

Said he would never leave me 'nor forsake me he saw the best in me, and because of him I have the victory.

Now I'm here the rest is history the Lord turned it around no more stress in me, praise Yah for blessing me.

Boy has he ever truly done a work in me finally
you can see the real zeal in me, working my
ministry prophesying the word of the Lord
accurately, yes factually.

No, it's not a hypocrisy, or democracy, it's a policy
of his majesty hierarchy. I Prophesy in spirit and in
truth it goes deep down to the very core of my
spiritual roots.

Suicide was on the enemy's hit list for my life
that is because he knew that I would eventually
dedicate my life to Christ.

So, his plots and plans resurfaced; he knows that
I'm worth it (priceless) I'm too much of a threat to
his kingdom, but my God reigns he, has dominion.

Thank you, Jesus for seeing the value in me
there's no devaluing me, add it up how many times
has he suffered and sacrificed it all for me?

I'm here to today because unlike man he never
gave up on me, locked me up and threw away the
key, I'm arrested and sanctified in thee.

Reflection Section

Write your thoughts down to express
how the poem made you think or feel.
Then reflect on them to see what you
can do to make a difference.

_____

_____

_____

_____

_____

_____

_____

_____

_____

_____

_____

_____

_____

_____

_____

_____

BACKSLIDER

You deserve the best don't allow yourself to be
abused and treated like the rest rich in love, can't
they smell the zest in which you possess?

Going through the motions going back and forth
rocking like an ocean falling victim to their potion,
it's obvious who's getting your devotion.

I'm focused!

This is bogus don't you know this?
I refuse to be used and abused by those who chose
to go back and slide behind enemy lines.

Thinking that is the way they'll beat the grind; it's
not really sublime to reach inside and listen to the
master's cry to prevent your demise, can't you see?
don't you realize?

Backslider,

It's time to wise up before your time winds down,
please don't be that clown, we don't want to frown
get on the right track who cares if some might say
that it's whack; I'm a fiend for Jesus Christ, yea it's
kinda like crack.

Here's a fact those who hear you hear me
they will not feel and no they will not bleed,
but, do right thing and heed me by planting the
right seeds.

Repent, and return unto the Lord for he is married
to the backslider this I'm sure, but, don't you want
to divorce yourself from the wicked ways of the
world?

Stop constantly giving into sin and the customs of
the enemy's games is that what you want to do, are
you willing to play and go astray?
Better think again and walk the other way.

Reflection Section

Write your thoughts down to express
how the poem made you think or feel.
Then reflect on them to see what you
can do to make a difference.

_____

_____

_____

_____

_____

_____

_____

_____

_____

_____

_____

_____

_____

_____

_____

_____

_____

MATERIAL WORLD

How many of you are really blind to what's going on in the world?

Visibly awake but consciously asleep; buying into the latest but not so greatest brand name clothes, do anything to get the gold even sell your souls. So many of them talk about I believe but yet they're thieves stealing truths, plus selling lies equals bad fruits, is that what we call, TRUE RELIGION?

Oh, VERSACE you think you got me with your snakes for long hair don't care? I don't think so, I won't stare deep into your traps for eyes that only work on the Men-tality to cause they're fatality, My God the calamity.

Isn't it amazing that LRG has so many people following them, look at the loyalty; even when our loved ones were sacrificed and hung from all types of trees, TIMBERLAND.

GUESS, what it's only a matter of time before they set the line and hook you in, where's the bait with all the hate for mankind.

NAUTICA so tell me who's really the B.O.S.S?

Get it together or it could be your loss.

LOUIS VUITTON got it going on,
enticed them with their LV strong,
 question is who's gonna pass the baton?

DOLCE & GABANA? Showing the people that
they prefer the banana using what God gave them
to please a sodomite's world and cease to multiply
they instead multiply the divide.

Sure, CHRISTIAN AUDIGIER isn't gay, but that
doesn't negate the fact that he promoted
blasphemy in some concealing type of way instead
of promoting YAH.

I hope and pray for his sake he gave his life to the
Lord before he passed away; or could it be that
DONNA KARAN is not so caring and please don't
ask me why (DKNY).

I'm wondering what do they really know about
SALVATORE FERRAGAMO? Okay, so maybe he
constructs well made belts that could perhaps whip
y'all into shape for the love that society has for
material possessions, the way that it has made a
way into your spiritual DNA.

Don't get mad or testy I'm only speaking what the Lord would have me say someone has got to do it, it's the only way to really spark the right human change.

Brand name attire won't get you into heaven and neither will your good works; the Father only looks at one thing, the abundance of heart it speaks the loudest.

What will it say on the day of judgment?, that they were great hosts? Left out the homeless just so they can post, toast, and take pictures in they're slave made clothes.

Reflection Section

Write your thoughts down to express how the poem made you think or feel. Then reflect on them to see what you can do to make a difference.

_____

_____

_____

_____

_____

_____

_____

_____

_____

_____

_____

_____

_____

_____

_____

_____

PART THREE

~

FAITH

KING

A man like this is hard to diss his presence is all supreme making moves, stays in school, while keeping cool that's why he's a king; destined for greatness, blessed with favor anointed vessel, is he.

Doing the works of the Lord while winning souls is the ultimate goal he still makes time for me, with the intent to better this world and the people that live therein.

Many are called but you were chosen, chosen to be king you passed the tests of many temptations due to tireless prayer and supplication. Possessing a unique sensation, is a prophet who will impact many different nations.

A man like this is hard to miss his presence is the golden light you see, he stems from true royalty, after all, his father is the original King of Kings.

Reflection Section

Write your thoughts down to express how the poem made you think or feel. Then reflect on them to see what you can do to make a difference.

_____

_____

_____

_____

_____

_____

_____

_____

_____

_____

_____

_____

_____

_____

_____

_____

QUEEN

A woman like this is hard to miss, her presence is the golden light you see; you look to admire and desire not her shape or her eyes, but the spirit of the Lord that lives inside.

There's something exceptionally special about her the way that she prays, lays, casts out demons , and the way that she slays in every which way.

This woman is anointed, blessed and highly favored she's sent from God, called to do many great things in the name of the Lord watch as she prevails and as she soars.

This woman has been ordained to excel in all that that she will do, ministers the gospel of Jesus Christ giving the people hope, giving them a real chance at life too.

Whatever her hands touch it will succeed afterall his majesty has already declared it to be.

A woman like this is hard to miss, her presence is the golden light you see; you look to admire and desire not her shape or her eyes, but the spirit of the Lord that lives inside.

Reflection Section

Write your thoughts down to express
how the poem made you think or feel.
Then reflect on them to see what you
can do to make a difference.

_____

_____

_____

_____

_____

_____

_____

_____

_____

_____

_____

_____

_____

_____

_____

_____

_____

FLEEK

Most of you go to the gym to work on getting it in
yet you slack on working out your prayer life;
busy getting physically fit, but your spiritually
weak in real life spirit man is lacking it's on visibly
sleep haven't you noticed it needs a physical tweak.

Focused on the wrong things got your priorities
mixed look to the Lord so you can go get those
things fixed man can't help you it'll always go
amiss. Change your ways can't you hear the sound
of the deep abyss?

Certainly, there must be better in mind for you
improving your life, spirit and soul too;
Think about what can bless you not stress you.

Barbells and treadmills can't and won't save you go
get a membership to your local spiritual gym it
won't cost anything for you my friend.

Work it out, get it in on your physical knees, your
flesh is on fleek, but your spirit man is on weak,
open your eyes people, it needs a visible tweak,
have you forgotten about your spiritual needs.

Is that really your hustle seven days of the week, isn't your eternal destination more important then temporary physication?

Do the math and read in between the lines, calculate your destiny's multiplication and the sensation of how many times the people obsess over the skin that we possess.

However, nonetheless we choose to reject the power that lies within deviating from the plan because of him (Satan) that leads to sin.

Trim the fat of lies so you can eat the fat of the land that has been intended for us by the Holy Lamb (Jesus). Skinny truths and big muscles does not glorify the father, the meek shall inherit the earth not the one with the better tan, hair like wool, or 401k plan.

Most of you go to the gym to work on getting it in yet you slack on working out your prayer life; busy getting physically fit, but your spiritually weak in real life spirit man is lacking it's on visibly sleep haven't you noticed it needs a physical tweak.

Reflection Section

Write your thoughts down to express how the poem made you think or feel. Then reflect on them to see what you can do to make a difference.

_____

_____

_____

_____

_____

_____

_____

_____

_____

_____

_____

_____

_____

_____

_____

_____

PLAYING (THE NAME) GAMES

If it's your intention to remove her draws that
means that you're still in the flesh because you
can't see past her; flaws, all you're really interested
in is being in between her thighs getting
hypnotized while trying to mesmerize.

Boy, you crazy you need to invest in a prayer shawl
and love this woman with your all because
anything bad formed against her will begin to fall;
down to your knees and proclaim she's queen.

Recognize that she's your heaven sent rib and no
it's not a fib, God is not a man that he should lie,
besides you can't deny the feeling inside as you
envision her in that white dress makes you wanna
cry.

'cause you know that she's a keeper so why do you
want to leave her open to another man's heart who
will recognize the Lord's plan to make that final
stand. You know you had the chance from the very
start.

Reflection Section

Write your thoughts down to express
how the poem made you think or feel.
Then reflect on them to see what you
can do to make a difference.

_____

_____

_____

_____

_____

_____

_____

_____

_____

_____

_____

_____

_____

_____

_____

_____

CHOSEN

There once was a time when I was lost in sin doing what I wanted that was way back when, but then I gave my life to Christ when he called me like Samuel in the middle of the night told me to get baptize while I was with child.

I could have been a fool and said in a while crocodile, but then it would've been a see ya later alligator.

Even in my sin I understood that obedience is better than sacrifice, so the next three weeks I really changed my strife listened to the Lord now I'm really living life.

It wasn't easy for me right away, but it was the best decision I could have ever made making the transition of walking astray from the path that was leading me away from the things of Yah.

Now I'm finally living a way pleasing to Yahweh, ministering to young men and women wherever I go; trying to be an example by things that I show. God has chosen me and set me apart anointed and graced; I have the Lord's mark.

Reflection Section

Write your thoughts down to express how the poem made you think or feel. Then reflect on them to see what you can do to make a difference.

_____
_____
_____
_____
_____
_____
_____
_____
_____
_____
_____
_____
_____
_____

_____
_____

MISSION TIME

I didn't know who I was because I had an identity crisis, until I came to the Lord now I truly know who Christ is.

So many times I had to work through the frustration never really was able to practice my concentration making the right demonstration by giving my life to God was truly the greatest celebration.

That's when the true fight began, I could see the infiltration through the separation and segregation of this tumultuous situation.
I'm on a different operation with sincere dedication to heal this wicked, broken, and nation.

It started with an imagination to caution the congregation, some of them have a secret organization forget the hesitation.

They're focusing on the sensation of they're future sexual penetration, talk about mind domination, such an abomination however, that's up to everyone's interpretation.

Time to win and save the souls of Yah before complete obliteration of the total population.

Hell is real and hell is hot you don't have to accept believe it or not for those who don't make it in will see it then what the saints were so called blabbering not to harbor in and not share, but minister the gospel to those who need and want to hear.

Forgive them Father for they know not what they do, they're lost souls trying to make it back to you, living their lives in sin is what they've grown accustomed to.

That's why you've sent out your soldiers in Christ to make sure they don't go astray.

"Come with me, I'll say, I'm going the other way".

Reflection Section

Write your thoughts down to express
how the poem made you think or feel.
Then reflect on them to see what you
can do to make a difference.

_____

_____

_____

_____

_____

_____

_____

_____

_____

_____

_____

_____

_____

_____

_____

_____

_____

DESTINY

God, I pray that you'll help keep me inspired
because you know I do it like no other
unfortunately, I can't say that I got it from my
mother, but I did get mine from my heavenly
Father (gifts).

They never even bothered to care when I chose to
share the things on my sleeve, the heart that I wear.
Exposing my deepest thoughts and feelings as if it
was transparent (underwear).

The Lord called me out from under there and led
me to the path of righteousness where you could
find the kind of treasures they wouldn't have in
stores, more blessings that's one thing for sure.

I prayed to God that I didn't have to pay a tuition
fee; sowed my seeds, my tuition was free. I give
thanks and praise to, Yeshua the almighty it was
meant to be.

Showed me the sign you see; yes it was my destiny,
that is how I knew he has truly called me into
ministry.

No more stressing and fighting it alone,

With God on my side I have Jehovah Shalom (peace).

Living like an alien I am not from this world I'm that one-of-a-kind, kind of girl never really fit into society's mold; No wonder, they couldn't contain the power that I hold.

Traveling on a uniquely made road, destined for greatness the prophecies untold it's just a matter of time before they unfold.

I'm here on an assigned mission, but Heaven's really my home I was sent to preach and teach the masses before life's final classes tests are marked; Covered with the blood of Jesus, destiny I'm His (child).

Operating with style you can see the favor, taste and see that the Lord is good, check out the flavor, it's sharper than a razor that's what you call a major trailblazer.

I am survivor and a thrivor raising up a new standard, CPR (reviver).

Reflection Section

Write your thoughts down to express
how the poem made you think or feel.
Then reflect on them to see what you
can do to make a difference.

_____

_____

_____

_____

_____

_____

_____

_____

_____

_____

_____

_____

_____

_____

_____

_____

FAITH

In our heart of hearts we know the truth, the truth about what you really do, being a child of God is no cake walk, it's a faith walk that's how we grew.

Living righteously in the Lord's sight, walking it out with all my might moving mountains is no fight, I pray to God and he makes it right everyday and every night.

Humbled myself and denied my plate focused on the love and not the hate; operating in my kingdom purpose because it's my fate.

Now is the time to focus on the Lord and consecrate, give your lives to God before it's too late.

Worship and praise is not a phase in which you go through; oh yes he owns you, it's a lifestyle, a journey we take for miles upon miles.

In Christ there's only authentic smiles like living in seclusion on a tropical Isle avoiding the Nile where there are wild crocodiles.

Seeking to devour like ravenous wolves be not deceived they don't look as how they should, they still can't hurt you even if they could.

You cannot trust everything that you hear, but please do not fear the Lord Yeshua is here to guide your every step, so don't fret the best is still yet to come no time to be so glum it will be enjoyable, it will all be so fun.

Faithing it with every fiber of your spiritual being are you finally seeing the goodness of the Lord in the land of the living, giving God praise showing him thanksgiving come on now, it's a given.

Reflection Section

Write your thoughts down to express
how the poem made you think or feel.
Then reflect on them to see what you
can do to make a difference.

_____
_____
_____
_____
_____
_____
_____
_____
_____
_____
_____
_____
_____

_____
_____

PART FOUR

~

LOVE

LOVE HURTS

One whole heart can easily become two
from red to blue how easy so soon
who thought, who knew.
I thought that we would be forever
living in love would be so clever
you and me being together.

Nothing truly lasts forever
as I've come to realize that one day we must part,
knowing this from the very start.

Trying to learn how to love again, being vulnerable
being hurts best friend, from the beginning to the
end.

I now know that this love thing wasn't cut out for
me because I try to be something, need something
that doesn't want me.

But, now I see ever so clear that life is,
was never meant to be fair, while feeling the snares
of everyone's stares.

Breaking me down one day at a time
losing at my best game, need to get in the right
frame.

Living in the darkness of night's first name
feels like my very own crime,
can't deny the feeling inside, living love's lie.

No friends, plenty foes
can't say yes, can't say no
should I stay or should I go
leave it be or let love flow?

Reflection Section

Write your thoughts down to express
how the poem made you think or feel.
Then reflect on them to see what you
can do to make a difference.

_____

_____

_____

_____

_____

_____

_____

_____

_____

_____

_____

_____

_____

_____

_____

_____

HANDS OF TIME

How could I turn back?...
The hands of time, the love I had for you was
unique, yes it was one of a kind.

But, you couldn't see that I was divine,
truly a diamond in disguise not something that
was so easy to find.
I guess I was too deep for you, the essence of my
being only blew your mind.

Do you really expect me to live my life on rewind,
put everything on pause until you decide that your
finally ready to settle down and press play.

Thought that it was cool and it was always going to
be that way, after you thought about it you barely
even said hey. You were going down a path that
was leading you astray.

I was more than willing to do my part
you had my love, you had my heart, but I guess the
wandering eyes kept you away; being out and
about was more important than being kept in, at
least with me you were still kept in.

How could I turn back?...

The hands of time, the love I had for you was
unique, yes it was one of a kind.

But, you couldn't see that I was divine,
truly a diamond in disguise not something that
was so easy to find..

I guess I was too deep for you, the essence of my
being only blew your mind.

Reflection Section

Write your thoughts down to express
how the poem made you think or feel.
Then reflect on them to see what you
can do to make a difference.

PASSION

I'm in love
I feel love
I share love
I can be love
I can tell when there is love
I can express love
I can tell you about me and love
I will show you love
I will let you feel love
I know you know when there is love,
but what is love?

Reflection Section

Write your thoughts down to express how the poem made you think or feel. Then reflect on them to see what you can do to make a difference.

_____

_____

_____

_____

_____

_____

_____

_____

_____

_____

_____

_____

_____

_____

_____

I THINK I'M IN LOVE

I think I'm in love with the way that he speaks to my soul, lets me know that God has everything in control.

The way that they drive me to places that I've never been before the meter has been measured at F for Full.

The constant anticipation of the mental simulation I think I'm in love. In love with the fact that the love he has for me is unconditional encourages me in ways like never before.

The joy in my heart cannot be explained and for that reason, I look forward to the day we share the same last name.

I think I'm in love, he always knows just what to say or do what a blessing he has been to me, drawing me in closer to God that's the way it's meant to be, a man that can lead.

I think I'm in love with all the possibilities and what this love could very well be; a ministry filled relationship based on the foundations of the bible and reinforcements of God.

I think I'm in love with the peace, joy, and happiness that I feel inside.

I know that the Lord is doing some amazing things with us right now preparing you for me and me for you.

This is the kind of love that I've only dreamt about, knew that I deserved but never thought that I would have.

How you love my children as if they were your own, spending time getting to know them making an effort to show that your love for me, for us is real.

I think I'm in love. I think I'm in love with you, flaws and all.

I am in love...

Reflection Section

Write your thoughts down to express
how the poem made you think or feel.
Then reflect on them to see what you
can do to make a difference.

_____
_____
_____
_____
_____
_____
_____
_____
_____
_____
_____

_____
_____

MERCY

The Savior of my life showed me mercy when he
quenched my thirsty gave me the only option of
the living water, I was on fire on the outside;
Now, I'm on fire on the inside eternally it's shut up
in my bones by the one who sits on the high of
highest thrones.

Not realizing the severity of the inferiority it was
kind of like joining a sorority making a pledge to
accept Jesus Christ into my life as my Lord was the
beginning for me; but truthfully it began a real
long time ago, (the day of Calvary).

When God gave his only begotten son, in these
modern day times like this, it was like he took three
bullets from a gun he was abused and crucified,
they shed his innocent blood.

He was wounded for our transgressions and
bruised for our iniquities took one for the team so
now we have the victory.

We break bread yes, he's been raised from the dead
he gave it all up for us, that was a necessary loss,
for us when he died on the cross for us.

It wasn't as easy as you think, raise our glasses let's
us drink in remembrance of the Lord, because of
him an eternal life is sure.

Given new grace and mercy so that we may live,
a gift of salvation, no condemnation or starvation;
I'm filled with the Holy Ghost he's always there for
me, always doing the most.

Making sure that I'm alright and taken cared of so
in turn I keep my vessel neat and clean, I'm such a
great host. (Selah)

Jesus never gave up on me when I wasn't doing
what I should have been I mean he could have
been but then where would I've been?

Have you ever seen someone dream of literally
giving their life to God?
Who would've thought it, that I'd be the one that
sought it, it couldn't have been that hard.

It's not a myth or some made up want or need I
mean get real on some highlight reel;
let's be honest did you see him bleed for our greed
or did he do it because he felt the need for his seed?

Trust me to be given the chance to glean from the most high supreme is the best feeling for a spiritual human being. Do you see where I'm going, do you now know what I mean?

There's nothing like the love of Christ (agape).
I'm his bride and on our wedding day they gave a different kind of rice, which was nice;
didn't look back, I didn't think twice.

Married the Man of dreams, now he's my eternal reality, I'm his Bride, Daughter, Servant, Queen (Mercy), Amen.

Reflection Section

Write your thoughts down to express
how the poem made you think or feel.
Then reflect on them to see what you
can do to make a difference.

_____

_____

_____

_____

_____

_____

_____

_____

_____

_____

_____

_____

_____

_____

_____

SUBMISSION

There's such a dissolution, but where's the
resolution and reconciliation?
We don't need a substitution, I'm talking about the
prostitution of the world's evolution.

Rebelling against the natural order of life.

God's word is sharper than a knife, it cut through
when he spoke; he said that it's not good for a man
to be alone, a man is supposed to take a wife.

 The husband is submitted unto Christ, the wife is
submitted unto her husband as she submits to his
instinctive lead, he submits to her every need; that's
the right way to do it!
one flesh, one team.

Christ is the head of the man, he has the ultimate
plan listen to his instructions that he gives you in
this land, he has plans to prosper you, not to harm
you, but give you hope and a future, it's not to
dupe ya.

So when he tells you husbands love your wives as
Christ loves the church, and wives honor your
husbands I promise it won't hurt; obey and heed
his commandments there's a reason he knows
everything first.

I promise to love you, honor and respect you
I might even challenge you, but only to bring out
the best in you; it's never my intention to test you
or disrespect you I only want to uplift you, edify
and protect you.

Some may say only a weak woman submits to a
man but it takes a special kind of man for God to
ordain that plan.

I believe it takes a strong but wise queen to submit
to her king's lead, she won't have to work him
hard, she won't ever have to plead.

Nor feel like she's begging it's not that type of
scheme; he's more than willing it's a part of their
regime.

The husband is submitted unto Christ, the wife is submitted unto her husband as she submits to his instinctive lead, he submits to her every need; that's the right way to do it!
one flesh, one team.

Reflection Section

Write your thoughts down to express
how the poem made you think or feel.
Then reflect on them to see what you
can do to make a difference.

_____

_____

_____

_____

_____

_____

_____

_____

_____

_____

_____

_____

_____

_____

_____

_____

ABORTION

Did you miss your Aunt?
I guess y'all couldn't get it together, it just didn't
Flo. Thought you were both so tight, make it past
anything it only seemed right.

What happened to waiting on her to come?
It was inevitable, she was always there for you that
wasn't anything new like that time when she
booked a flight, came out of nowhere and just
showed up while you were at school...
so embarrassing.

Eventually, you got used to her showing up
unannounced crossing your fingers it wouldn't be
at your prom, after-all you and your friends had
plans to slow dance with some guys.

Somehow you ended up in a trance, he must have
spiked your punch and such; things followed up as
you fell down into this unknown man's bed, now
he's being aggressive he's trying to force you to
give him some h**d.

Took something from you ever so priceless,
no receipt, no returns, non-refundable, he stole
your purity and innocence in a two-for-one (no
deal).

You want to scream thief, I mean rapist, but you
can't you feel so weak. What did he give you? Your
feeling tipsy and falling asleep you can't run, you
can't leave.

Your friend is there trying to stop it, but the other
guy won't let her so now she felt defeat.

Finally, it's over and you go back home nobody
knows anything, you haven't said a peep.

Why did this happened to me? you ask yourself
I'm basically a kid, I'm only in high school.
But that didn't stop him, he wanted a piece, the
thing is I didn't have anything to give,
I wasn't selling pie or whatever he thought was his.

He should be ashamed of himself, but how?, when
he clearly has no conscience.
What do you mean?, he drugged me and I became
UN-conscious or did he always have that in the
back of his mind, (sub-conscious).

Months go by and I still think about that night, I was so mad at myself I could barely put up a fight, I couldn't shake what happened it just wasn't right.

And to make matters worse my Aunt Flo whom I have a love-hate relationship with hasn't even come to see me in months.

At first I didn't think it was anything to be too concerned about because she's always been finicky with me, but then it seemed as though she really wasn't checking for me.

No, there's no way she just decided to up and leave me like that, I know I complained about her coming around unannounced she must have taken it personal, because I don't see her anymore.

Is there something wrong with me, no it couldn't be, this hasn't happened before; I have to find out, I need to know for sure I cannot see how could this be? I mean I'm still a "v", I think?

Here she is at the doctors with a cup in hand, she's told to go the washroom to go pee hoping it's negative, wouldn't that be a relieve.

Pregnancy test is there we're waiting to see why
has my, Aunt Flo just forsaken thee
The doctor finally comes in and asks me is
everything okay? How have you been?

She said, look at me I'm a mess I'm about to take
my finals, about to take my test this is the last thing
I need. He then looks at me and says, I understand
I know what you mean; I look at him like he's
crazy, after-all he hasn't been where I've been or
seen what I've seen.

The doctor tells her that she is pregnant, here she is
worried about school she didn't flunk the test, she
got a 100% is what it read, that she going to be a
mother; congratulations he said.

She immediately, fainted she thought she was
dead, getting all hyped up she thought it was the
end.

Arriving back to her house as she's walking in the
door, and now she's crying her tears are streaming
down her face as they hit the tiled floor
what will she ever do, she had to think quick in a
few months she would be due.

The thoughts of abortion had really plagued her
mind, but, I'm a Christian this is God's creation, the
work of the Lord; My God this is truly sublime
I can't abort this baby, this baby is mine.
quite a difficult decision to be face with.

It's not like we can rewind the hands of time
(timeless) and change the scenario all while
listening to God's voice through the music stereo.

Heard a song that sang, "the best is yet to come
(DA DA, DA, Dum), loving on that baby boy he's
the one, nothing could change what I have for you.
No more moonshine rum, the past is over, embrace
your soon to be son. It means so much more, they
might talk, but there's blessings galore in-store".

Yes, Lord I hear you loud and its ever so clear
Nothing can separate us from his love, I swear.

So, I decided to give his life a chance he deserved it
because, God said that he knew us before we were
formed in our mother's womb, as hard as it could
be he knew that I wouldn't do it; he knew that he
knew.

Thank you, Jesus for speaking to me.

Abortion is so not cool, killing an innocent life
might be acceptable for some of you, but not for me
I learned my lessons and I pray to God you all will
too.

Reflection Section

Write your thoughts down to express
how the poem made you think or feel.
Then reflect on them to see what you
can do to make a difference.

_____

_____

_____

_____

_____

_____

_____

_____

_____

_____

_____

_____

_____

_____

_____

_____

PART FIVE

~

RELATIONSHIPS

I'M TIRED

I'm tired of the non-stop bickering.

I'm tired of fighting.

I'm tired of pretending that I'm happy when I'm clearly not.

I'm tired of being put down and ridiculed every single day.

I'm tired of being called nasty hurtful names.

I'm tired of hurting mentally, physically and emotionally.

I'm tired of being neglected.

I'm tired of being told that I'm not worthy.

I'm tired of you.

I'm tired of feeling held back.

I'm tired of everything.

I am so much more than what you think I am.

I am beautiful, strong, motivated, determined, smart, creative, intelligent, insatiable and inspiring. I am a Black Queen, a Nubian empress.

I AM ME!!!

Reflection Section

Write your thoughts down to express
how the poem made you think or feel.
Then reflect on them to see what you
can do to make a difference.

_____

_____

_____

_____

_____

_____

_____

_____

_____

_____

_____

_____

_____

_____

_____

_____

SOUL TIES

Soul ties are like phone lines forever there and ever clear, not like the reception even in it's unfair deception there's always a cost.

Long distance fees or a bundled package of the false conception is the misconception, that it would be best for me making the assumption that it would be different than the last was my fault you see.

Good thing for Christ it's a toll-free, call thee; God is on the speed dial The Father, The Son & The Holy Spirit are the Trinity he's on it like 1,2,3

Yes, the soul tie is like the phone line it had been broken, now I'm finally free.

Reflection Section

Write your thoughts down to express
how the poem made you think or feel.
Then reflect on them to see what you
can do to make a difference.

TRUST

Trust is more than just a five letter word,
it means much more to most people who take pride
in saying that it's bond, but for how long?
Does it hold value, is it really strong?

How much is it worth to you?
kind of like the woman who gave birth to you;
Priceless and would do anything to protect it,
never neglect it surely you wouldn't disrespect it.

Would you suspect it from those that you trust
if it's broken then is it a total bust?
Are you willing to mend and sustain it
or accept the blame in complete disdain
sensing the stain of the mistrust.

We only have trust when you and I become US,
how could anyone ever be so vulnerable, when the
ones you love try to set you up, no not for
greatness.

Do you hear the sound of the trumpets? Who's
been selected from the Twelve Tribes of Israel, Oh
wait! my memory is coming back, the story of
Joseph I remember all too well (Manasseh).

Reflection Section

Write your thoughts down to express how the poem made you think or feel. Then reflect on them to see what you can do to make a difference.

_____

_____

_____

_____

_____

_____

_____

_____

_____

_____

_____

_____

_____

_____

DIAMOND IN THE ROUGH

I'm the diamond in the rough that everyone seems
blind to. You'd be so blessed if you even knew who
you were really talking to, not trying to school you,
but I just thought I would give you the chance to
say I knew you.

They say that a diamond is a girl's best friend well,
I don't know how true that could be because I'm
the girl that was ignored like the English pound
but everyone wanted the Yen.

The bona fide one of a kind true type of friend,
I don't flex with everyone not because I think I'm
the better one, but because I'm a son of God,
anointed not trying to blend in.

Set apart I have his mark, the mark of the most
high and I won't be denied because I know who
supplies all my needs, he gave it all for me He saw
the best in me, boy did he ever see.

I am a diamond in the rough even the Lord called
my bluff when I tried to act so tough;
he let me know that he would never leave me 'nor
forsake me now I'm really shining, ever so
blinding.
They say that a diamond is a girl's best friend,

well I don't know how true that could be because,
I'm the girl that was ignored like the English
pound, but everyone wanted the Yen.

I'm genuine and authentic sometimes even a little
eccentric, but, I don't deal with cubic zirconia
friendships, fake or make believe, I know what I've
seen, call it pretend.

Zero clarity I'm definitely not into the popularity
I desire the real deal Holy-field, no en-(Tyson).

There's no contemplating just demonstrating what
purposeful connections are supposed to look like,
motivating not so dominating, encouraging feeling
the energy of love surging.

Divine and always on time some sent by God, and
some from the fraud slimy and grimy don't kiss
that frog.

They say that a diamond is a girl's best friend,
well I don't know how true that could be because,
I'm the girl that was ignored like the English
pound, but everyone wanted the Yen.

Reflection Section

Write your thoughts down to express how the poem made you think or feel. Then reflect on them to see what you can do to make a difference.

_____

_____

_____

_____

_____

_____

_____

_____

_____

_____

_____

_____

_____

_____

_____

GRAND MASTER THOUGHTS

There's nothing quite like being yourself living up
to the expectations of God, and not of man's,
recognizing the master's ordained plans.

Trying to live righteously in God's sight
doing my best with all my might while the wicked
party and drink all day and night.

But, you see we all fall short of his wonderful glory,
I know that is true because its apart of my very
own story. It's not an excuse it's an
acknowledgment of the trials and tribulation of our
bewilderment.

No, it's not something that we can easily blame on
this corrupted government; undercover men acting
like Victoria Secret Service or Maybelline's
Foundation to cover up their sins even the ones
from way back when.

With the not so blemish free monopoly system,
operating in such a way that they started dissing
the malnutrition families; they were supposed to be
protected by the so called democracy,
clearly those were lies, hypocrisy.

Reflection Section

Write your thoughts down to express
how the poem made you think or feel.
Then reflect on them to see what you
can do to make a difference.

_____

_____

_____

_____

_____

_____

_____

_____

_____

_____

_____

_____

_____

_____

_____

_____

_____

_____

VIRTUOUS WOMAN

You gotta make sure that you marry a praying kind of woman; a Proverbs 31 kind of woman, provides for her family, a well respected kind of woman.

She gets up early to seek the Lord's face kind of woman; sometimes even without brushing her teeth or washing her face 'cause she was in such a haste kind of woman.

Don't disgrace this kind of woman a, godly type of woman, the kind who'll go out her way for her children and husband kind of woman.

She's a virtuous God fearing woman; a blessed and highly anointed type of woman. Stands in the gap and intercede on your behalf kind of woman, can you sense this kind of woman?

Knows how to make something of nothing; she'll build you up kind of woman. Contains power and super favor this right here woman.

She will speak life in and over you kind of woman; You can call her a one of a kind, virtuous, glory and grace filled type of woman.

Reflection Section

Write your thoughts down to express
how the poem made you think or feel.
Then reflect on them to see what you
can do to make a difference.

_____

_____

_____

_____

_____

_____

_____

_____

_____

_____

_____

_____

_____

_____

THESE KEYS

I gave you the keys to my heart, but you gave them
back to me I was hurt and brokenhearted because
you wanted to walk away from me.

I then knew that you weren't the one for me,
we barely spent time together we hardly ever had
fun you see.

We shared more than a few laughs, some that
made me crack up then there were times when you
called me out my name maybe you thought it was
funny, perhaps you though it was a game.

Hurting the only woman that ever really loved you
only makes you look lame; truly is such a shame
how when I look back I wonder was it worth the
headache, was it even worth the pain?

But God,

He came and gave me the keys to life
I'm no longer worried about being your wife
I am already loved by the one who gives me life as
a Bride of Christ.

No more tears, no more hurt, no more pain from
the one who made me cry for unknown reasons I
guess I'll never really know why.

Now, you will get to see someone else treat me
right the way you were supposed to all those days
and all those nights.

I've had myself guarded and hidden from man's
sight kept away for such a time as this
to eventually be revealed to the one who has been
chosen by the Almighty's right hand.

Lord knows he's the right man he'll protect me,
fight for me and do his best with all his might.

Only this time God gave the keys to the one who
would unlock my heart, eternally together we will
never part for I am this man's future wife
talk about this real love, no more strife.

Reflection Section

Write your thoughts down to express how the poem made you think or feel. Then reflect on them to see what you can do to make a difference.

_____

_____

_____

_____

_____

_____

_____

_____

_____

_____

_____

_____

_____

_____

_____

FORNICATOR

Do you like the way it feels when your body parts
gets hard as steel? When she's slippery than a
water slide as you try to reach deep inside, deep
into her soul is that really your goal?

You think she's some amusement ride at 6 flags
that you can explore, by searching her grounds for
the next climax, trying to get up close like a 3D I
max.

I've got news for you brother there's things in store
the fact that you've bound yourself to this woman
for years and more not the way you were thinking,
this I'm sure, (Soul Ties).

Brethren, not only do you grieve the Father in
Heaven, and tether in as he watches you defile his
daughter's glory what do you think will come of
this story?

No punishment for tainting another man's future
wife before she had the time to say I do to the one
whom submits to the Most High.
Who sits high and looks low on all things that goes
on in this world,

so think not for a moment that you go unnoticed to
the one who sees it all.

Young woman don't you know who you are and
who's you are?

That you ought to be cherished by the one I have
for you, created and prepared for you don't let this
world come around and try to be tainting you,
infiltrating you, berating you, they're not even
interested in saving you only disgracing you and
shaming you.

Shame on you!

You're fearfully and wonderfully made in my
image, fashioned after thee, don't you see that I
want you to live victoriously through me?

My children come hither and listen closely,
I tell you these things, you mostly because you do
not see what will be if you do not listen to me and
heed my warning.

Verily I say unto you that no fornicators, nor
thieves, nor covetous, nor drunkards, nor revilers,
nor swindlers will inherit the Kingdom of Heaven.

Giving it all up to a man or woman that isn't your spouse is exactly how you'll end up with louse.

Be patient and wait on the Lord he's always on time and never late, plus it's worth heaven's rewards or would you prefer Satan's lure to your destruction; opposed to your destiny's fate.

There's no need for rushing or private part touching, you're not missing out on nothing except the enemy's infiltration of sexual temptation.

I do my due diligence to practice what I preach, are you even listening to the words that I speak?

I'm not out here doing dirt, I'm out here winning souls in these crooked streets being about my father's business there's people I have to teach. If you don't learn there's a possibility that you could burn.

You need to pass this test;
Yes, it's your turn.

Reflection Section

Write your thoughts down to express
how the poem made you think or feel.
Then reflect on them to see what you
can do to make a difference.

_____

_____

_____

_____

_____

_____

_____

_____

_____

_____

_____

_____

_____

_____

_____

ACKNOWLEDGMENTS

I'd like to thank all the people who have supported and encouraged me along the way. I'd also like to thank my three amazing, beautiful and gifted children for inspiring me and keeping me on my toes, I love you so much.

And lastly, I'd like to acknowledge the dreamers, believers, and lost souls, you have also motivated me to do more; all I ask is that you never give up and always keep your eyes on God. I also charge you to be bold as a lion, knowing that you have Jesus on your side never to leave or forsake you. The Lord showed me that my purpose was to spark a light and ignite a change in this world. I knew that my poetry would be a small start to what will be, a mighty and powerful movement. So, let's bring it back to the source of it all, God; for he is worthy of all praise and glory because without him, we are nothing.

ABOUT THE AUTHOR

Danielle Bailey is a poet, writer, speaker and entrepreneur. However, her passion is helping people recognize their potential, while realizing their worth.

Danielle's mission is to breakdown strongholds and build-up strong souls whereby exceeding beyond the four walls. She's a minister and founder of UNQLY MADE Ministries International.

Her message transcends barriers with it's deep healing and impacting poetic delivery, that sparks change and inspires deliverance in the body of Christ. She is truly emulating what, "Married to Ministry" is all about.

BOOKS BY DANIELLE BAILEY

Quotes From The Soul, To Help Heal A Queen's Heart: 31-Day Inspirational

Poetics- A Prophetic Poetry Devotional: On Life, Love, And Relationships To Help Keep You Spiritually Fit!

www.ingramcontent.com/pod-product-compliance
Lightning Source LLC
La Vergne TN
LVHW091153080426
835509LV00006B/670